7/02

W9-BHG-502

MIDLOTHIAN
PUBLIC LIBRARY

101 Facts About PETS
101 Facts About

101 FACTS ABOUT

HAMSTERS

Please visit our web site at: www.garethstevens.com
For a free color catalog describing Gareth Stevens Publishing's list of high-quality books and multimedia programs, call 1-800-542-2595 (USA) or 1-800-461-9120 (Canada). Gareth Stevens Publishing's Fax: (414) 332-3567.

Library of Congress Cataloging-in-Publication Data

Barnes, Julia.
    101 facts about hamsters / by Julia Barnes. — North American ed.
      p. cm. — (101 facts about pets)
    Includes bibliographical references and index.
    Summary: Provides information about different kinds of hamsters, how to care for them, and how to understand their behavior.
    ISBN 0-8368-3018-0 (lib. bdg.)
    1. Hamsters as pets—Miscellanea—Juvenile literature. [1. Hamsters—Miscellanea.]
    I. Title: One hundred one facts about hamsters. II. Title. III. Series.
    SF459.H3B35   2002
    636.9'356—dc21   2001049494

This North American edition first published in 2002 by
Gareth Stevens Publishing
A World Almanac Education Group Company
330 West Olive Street, Suite 100
Milwaukee, WI 53212 USA

This U.S. edition © 2002 by Gareth Stevens, Inc. Original edition © 2001 by Ringpress Books Limited. First published by Ringpress Books Limited, P.O. Box 8, Lydney, Gloucestershire, GL15 4YN, United Kingdom. Additional end matter © 2002 by Gareth Stevens, Inc.

Ringpress Series Editor: Claire Horton-Bussey
Ringpress Designer: Sara Howell
Gareth Stevens Editors: Jim Mezzanotte and Mary Dykstra

Printed in Hong Kong through Printworks Int. Ltd

1 2 3 4 5 6 7 8 9 06 05 04 03 02

101 Facts About

PETS

101 Facts About

101 FACTS ABOUT

HAMSTERS

Julia Barnes

Gareth Stevens Publishing
A WORLD ALMANAC EDUCATION GROUP COMPANY

1 The hamster is the most popular of small pets. These creatures are easy to care for, and they are also lots of fun to watch.

2 Hamsters get their name from the German word "hamstern," which means "to **hoard**," or hide away to use later. A hamster carries food in its cheeks, then hoards the food underground.

3 The hamster belongs to a family of animals called **rodents**. Mice, rats, gerbils, and guinea pigs are also rodents.

4 More than twenty kinds of hamsters live in the wild, but only a few kinds have been **domesticated**, or tamed and kept as pets.

5 The Syrian, or Golden, hamster (opposite, top) comes from the deserts of Syria, in the Middle East. This creature is the most common hamster kept as a pet.

6 Hamsters are **nocturnal**, which means they sleep during the day and are active at night.

7 Although hamsters are very small, in the wild they travel long distances searching for food. Wild hamsters can travel more than 12 miles (19 kilometers) in one night.

8 In the wild, hamsters eat seeds, green leaves, and some insects, and they carry food home by using the pouches they have in their cheeks. Syrian hamsters can carry up to half their own body weight in food inside their pouches.

9 Wild hamsters live in the ground in **burrows**. A burrow has many different "rooms" and can be 3 feet (1 meter) underground.

10 One hundred years ago, people thought there were no more Syrian hamsters, but in 1932 a scientist discovered a female hamster and her babies in the Syrian desert. Today, all Syrian hamsters kept as pets come from this family.

11 The Syrian hamster is about 6 inches (15 centimeters) long. The female Syrian hamster is larger than the male.

12 A Syrian hamster will usually live for about two years. Some Syrian hamsters live longer, however, reaching up to four years of age.

13 In the wild, Syrian hamsters can be quite fierce. Wild Syrian hamsters often fight with each other.

14 Pet Syrian hamsters will also fight each other. You should only keep one Syrian hamster in a cage at one time.

15 Unlike the Syrian hamster, which likes to live alone, dwarf hamsters like to live in pairs. Keep either two males or two females together. The dwarf hamster is smaller than the Syrian hamster.

16 The Dwarf Chinese hamster (left) is still found in the wild in eastern Europe and Asia. A Dwarf Chinese hamster measures about 4 inches (10 cm) long. Dwarf Chinese hamsters usually live 18 months to 2 years.

18 The Dwarf Winter White Russian hamster comes from Siberia and northern Asia, where it often snows. Winter whites are about 3 inches (8 cm) long and live for 18 months to 2 years.

17 In the wild, the Dwarf Campbell's Russian hamster (above) lives in the sand dunes of northern Russia, central Asia, and China. This hamster measures 3 to 4 inches (8 to 10 cm) long and lives about two years.

19 All the varieties of dwarf hamsters move very quickly and are more difficult to handle than the Syrian hamsters.

20 The Roborovski hamster (right) is the smallest dwarf hamster kept as a pet. Measuring just 2 inches (5 cm) long, this lively but tiny creature needs a lot of special care.

21 Although the Syrian hamster is famous for its golden color, today Syrian hamsters come in about 100 varieties of colors.

22 Hamsters that are almost all one color are called **"selfs"** and come in a wide range of golds and browns, from the palest cream to the deepest honey. These hamsters also come in silver-blue, chocolate, lilac, and black varieties.

23 Syrian hamsters can have different eye colors, too. A Syrian hamster might have a cream coat with red eyes or a cream coat with black eyes.

24 Syrian hamsters can also have any one of these coat patterns:

- **banded**: a colored coat with a white band across the back and stomach
- **roan**: a white coat, but with colored hairs throughout the coat
- **dominant spot**: a white coat with colored spots on it, except on the stomach
- **piebald**: a white coat, but with spots and patches of color throughout the coat

25 Most Syrian hamsters have short-haired coats. Some Syrian hamsters,

however, have other kinds of coats:

- long-haired (above), also known as "teddy bear" or "angora"
- rex: hair that is slightly curled and rough
- satin: hair that is smooth, shiny, and silky

26 **Breeders**, or people who raise hamsters, have developed a hamster that has no hair. It is called an Alien hamster.

27 Dwarf hamsters are not as colorful as Syrian hamsters. The Dwarf Chinese hamster (below) is usually chestnut brown, with gray ears and a black stripe down its back.

28 Dwarf Campbell's Russian hamsters have a brown-gray coat with a dark brown stripe down the back. Other dwarf hamster colors include the following:

- albino: pure white with red eyes
- opal: a blue-gray color
- argente: a rich orange color with a brown-gray stripe down the back

29 Dwarf hamsters can have different coat patterns. A dwarf hamster's coat can be mottled (white with patches or spots of color) or platinum (silver).

30 Dwarf Campbell's Russian hamsters usually have short-haired coats, but they can also have satin or wavy-haired coats.

31 Dwarf Winter White Russian hamsters have dark gray coats with a black stripe down the back.

32 In the wild, a Dwarf Winter White Russian hamster will turn white in the winter, so it can blend in with the snowy landscape.

33 Breeders have developed a Dwarf Winter White Russian hamster (left) that is sapphire (purple-gray) and has a gray stripe running down its back.

34 Roborovski hamsters, the smallest of the dwarf hamsters, only come in one color. They are sandy-colored with white stomachs.

35 If you want to keep a hamster as a pet, you should visit a pet store, where the staff can help you choose a hamster.

36 You can also visit a breeder, who will have special varieties of hamsters with different colors and patterns.

37 Try to visit the pet store in the late afternoon or early evening, so you can see the hamsters in action. Remember, they sleep during the day and are active at night.

38 When selecting a hamster, first decide whether you want to keep a male or a female hamster. Males and females both make good pets.

13

39 The staff at the pet store should be able to answer any questions you might have. They can also help you pick out a hamster that is right for you.

40 Buy a hamster that is between five and ten weeks old, so the animal is easy to handle and train.

41 When you choose a hamster, make sure to look for the signs of good health shown below.

coat: soft and clean

eyes: bright and clear, with no discharge

nose: clean and free of discharge

body: well rounded

mouth: clean, with no sign of dribbling

42 Before buying a hamster, you must decide where it will live in your house. A hamster will need to live in a room that has a temperature between 68° and 72° Fahrenheit (20° and 22° Celsius).

43 If the temperature drops below 50°F (10°C), a hamster will curl up and go into a deep sleep, and the animal will not wake up until the temperature has risen again.

44 Just like people, hamsters can catch colds. Make sure your pet is not exposed to any drafts of air, which can enter through a window or door.

45 Make sure your pet is out of direct sunlight and away from heat vents. Your hamster should also be in a place where it can sleep undisturbed.

47 Multistory cages are dangerous for dwarf hamsters because the animals can slip and fall. If you decide to keep a dwarf hamster, choose a smaller glass or plastic tank (below).

48 No matter the size, the hamster cage needs a tight-fitting lid to keep your pet from escaping.

46 Hamster cages come in many shapes and sizes. If you decide to keep a Syrian hamster, get a multistory plastic unit (above), so your pet has an interesting home to live in with lots of places to explore.

because it may irritate the hamster's eyes.

51 Provide your pet with water in a bottle that can clip to its cage.

52 Gravity-fed water bottles, which can be purchased at a pet store, allow smaller pets such as hamsters to sip water from a small metal tube (below).

49 Inside the cage, your hamster will need a nesting box, which is where it sleeps. Provide your pet with paper towels or shredded tissues, which it will use to line the inside of the box.

50 Cover the bottom of your hamster's cage with 2 to 3 inches (5 to 8 cm) of soft wood shavings, which you should be able to buy from a pet store. Do not use sawdust,

53 A pet store will carry a variety of toys for your hamster – tunnels for exploring, ladders and ramps for climbing, and wheels for exercise sessions.

54 The cheapest toys are often the best. Try using the cardboard tube from inside a toilet paper roll as a toy. Your hamster will have fun going in and out of the tube and will then enjoy chewing on the cardboard!

55 Hollow plastic balls are fun toys that provide your hamster with exercise. These hamster balls come in many sizes. Never leave your hamster on its own when it is playing in a toy of this kind.

56 Your hamster will need time to explore its cage after you bring it home. Give your pet a few days to settle in before you try to handle it.

lift your pet, then hold it with your hands cupped. Speak softly to your hamster as you handle it, so it gets to know your voice.

57 After a few days, try gently touching your hamster while it is in its new home, so the animal gets used to your smell. Then give your pet some food, such as a piece of lettuce, so it starts to trust you.

59 Sit down when you are handling your hamster, so if your pet jumps or wiggles loose, it will land in your lap.

58 After your hamster has taken food from your hand, try picking up the animal. Use both hands to

61 If you have other pets in your home, such as a cat or dog, make sure they are in another room when you take your hamster out of its cage.

60 Make sure your hamster does not run loose when it is playing. Hamsters are very tiny and fast, and they can quickly squeeze into the smallest of places. If a hamster gets loose, it can cause a lot of damage and even hurt itself. It will chew on furniture and also gnaw electrical wires.

62 You should feed your hamster a mixture of seed, grain, and nuts, which you can buy at a pet store.

20

63 Your pet can also be fed a hamster food that comes in pellet form.

64 Put your hamster's food in a heavy, shallow bowl that will hold what your pet eats in a day. Be sure the animal can reach the bottom of the bowl.

65 Make sure that you store your hamster's food in a dry place inside your house. If the seed mix is allowed to get damp, it can become moldy or stale and might then cause your pet to get sick.

66 You can also give your hamster small amounts of chopped fruit and vegetables. Hamsters usually like carrots, broccoli, apples, and oranges, as well as tiny chunks of cheese.

67 Wash all fruits and vegetables before feeding them to your pet.

68 For a special treat, you can give your hamster peanuts in the shell, as well as raisins and pieces of dog biscuit.

69 Remove uneaten food from your hamster's bowl every day. You should also look for any food your pet may have hidden in its sleeping area.

70 If you watch the different ways your hamster behaves, you will begin to understand what your pet is feeling.

71 Teeth chattering is a sign that your hamster is upset. Do not touch it if you hear this sound. You may get bitten.

72 Hamsters will stand on their hind legs to listen more closely to an interesting sound. They have very good hearing.

73 Dwarf hamsters communicate with each other through high-pitched squeaks that we cannot hear.

74 When a Syrian hamster screams at a high pitch, the animal is very frightened.

75 Your hamster will only use one area of its cage as a bathroom, so that the rest of the cage stays clean.

76 To provide your hamster with a toilet, place a small jar on its side in the cage. You can also use a small tin lid.

77 You should put a small amount of cat litter or sand in the jar or lid that your hamster is using for a toilet. Be sure to clean this toilet daily.

78 A hamster will clean its coat by licking its front paws and then using them like tiny washcloths. The animal will sometimes use the claws on its back paws to comb its fur.

81 A hamster's teeth grow all the time, but they wear down naturally if the animal has something to chew. Gnawing blocks are available at most pet stores.

79 If you are keeping a long-haired Syrian hamster, you will need to clean its coat. Try gently brushing the coat with a soft toothbrush (above).

80 Provide your dwarf Russian hamster with a small dish filled with sand. The animal will roll in the dish to clean grease off of its coat.

82 If your hamster's teeth do become too long, you may need to take it to a **veterinarian**, or animal doctor, who will cut your pet's teeth.

83 Your hamster's nails should wear down naturally, but if they get too long, ask a veterinarian to clip them.

84 Pay close attention to your hamster's appearance and behavior. If a hamster that is usually friendly tries to bite, or if the animal stops eating or loses weight, it is probably sick and should see a veterinarian.

85 If you need to visit a veterinarian, put your pet in a plastic carrying box (right). You can also use a small cardboard box that has holes to let in air. Place bedding in the box so your pet has a comfortable ride.

86 Try not to handle your hamster if you have a cold, as it could catch your cold. A hamster with a cold will have a runny nose and watery eyes and will sneeze. Take your pet to a veterinarian if it has a cold.

88 Hamsters can also suffer from allergies to certain foods or bedding. If your pet has watery eyes and is sneezing, it may be allergic to something in its cage or in its diet.

87 Tiny animals called **mites** sometimes live inside a hamster's ears or on the skin around its head. If your hamster keeps scratching its head, it may have mites. A veterinarian can get rid of mites if your pet has them.

89 If a hamster is wet around its tail, it may have an infection called "wet tail." Wet tail causes diarrhea and can be fatal. If you think your pet has wet tail, you should take it to a veterinarian immediately.

90 Before putting a male and female hamster together, be sure you can find homes for any young they might produce.

91 A male Syrian hamster will not take care of its young. In fact, a male Syrian hamster is usually kept away from its young, so the babies can stay safe.

young warm when the female is away from the nest.

92 Male dwarf hamsters are very involved with their families. A male dwarf hamster brings food to his young and keeps his

93 If a female hamster is expecting babies, she should be given extra nesting material so she can build a nest.

96 A **litter** of hamsters usually averages seven or eight pups, but it can be larger.

97 The record for the largest litter of pet hamsters is 26 pups, born in 1974 in Louisiana.

94 A female hamster is pregnant for only 16 to 18 days before giving birth to her babies.

95 Baby hamsters are born blind and without hair. They are called puppies, or pups.

100 For the first two weeks, a pup drinks its mother's milk. Then it eats finely chopped food. A pup can leave its mother after about three weeks.

98 For the first few weeks of the pups' lives, the nest should not be disturbed, or the female may get upset and kill her babies.

99 Hamster pups grow very quickly. By the time they are a week old the young hamsters have hair, and their eyes open after about two weeks.

101 If you keep a pet hamster, it will become part of your family. You will have fun watching your pet and giving it lots of special care.

Glossary

banded: a Syrian hamster coat with a white band across the back and stomach.

breeder: a person who raises and keeps a certain kind of animal, such as a hamster.

burrows: holes in the ground that animals use for shelter.

domesticated: not wild, and comfortable living with humans.

dominant spot: a Syrian hamster coat that is white with colored spots throughout, except on the stomach.

hoard: to collect and hide away for future use.

litter: a group of baby animals born at the same time to the same mother.

mites: tiny insects that live and feed on a plant or an animal.

nocturnal: to be active at night and asleep during the day.

piebald: a Syrian hamster coat that is white with colored spots and patches.

roan: a Syrian hamster coat that is white but has colored hairs all through it.

rodent: a member of a group of animals, including hamsters, rats, mice, and gerbils, that gnaw with their front teeth.

selfs: hamsters that are almost all one color.

veterinarian: a doctor whose job is making sure that animals stay healthy.

More Books to Read

Hamster (ASPCA Pet Care Guides for Kids series)
Mark Evans (DK Publishing)

Hamsters
Otto Von Frisch
(Econo-Clad Books)

Starting with Hamsters
Georg Gassner
(Econo-Clad Books)

The Really Useful Hamster Guide
Lorraine Hill
(TFH Publications)

Web Sites

All About Hamsters
www.allabouthamsters.com

Hamster Hideout
www.hamsterhideout.com

Hamsterific
www.hamsterific.com

Hamsters
www.surfnetkids.com/hamsters.htm

To find additional web sites, use a reliable search engine, such as www.yahooligans.com, with one or more of the following keywords: **hamsters, pet rodents, hamster care.**

Index